*Janet,
Thank you for
love + support!*
JoAnn

PONDER THIS
Just a Bit of Inspiration

JoAnn Wilson

Published By:
CRBarton Productions, LLC
P.O. Box 962
Reisterstown, Maryland 21136
www.crbarton.com

This book is a work of the opinion of the author and any references or similarities to actual events, real people, living or dead, or to real places, are intended to give the novel a sense of reality. Any similarities in names, characters, places and incidents are entirely coincidental.

Scripture quotations are taken from the Holy Bible, New International Version ®, Copyright© 1984 by the International Bible Society, Used by Permission of Zondervan Publishing House. All Rights Reserved.

Scripture quotations in this publication are from the New King James Version and authorized by New King James Version.

No part of this publication may be reproduced, stored in a retrieval system or transmitted in any form or by any means, including, but not limited to electronically, mechanical recording or photocopying without prior written permission of the publisher and author. For permission requests, contact the publisher at the mailing or email address above.

Ordering Information:
Quantity sales: Special discounts are available on quantity purchases by corporations, associations and others. For details, contact the publisher.

Copyright © 2017 JoAnn Wilson
All rights reserved.
ISBN: 0-9978779-8-7
ISBN-13: 978-0-9978779-8-4

Introduction

Do you ever find yourself in need of a word of encouragement? Is there someone special you can go to who may understand how you feel when times are tough? Have you wanted to hear it's okay - you're okay?

Hopefully, what you will find in this book are things to ponder on as you traverse this journey of life. There are notes, phases and scriptures that I pray will inspire, encourage and challenge you to look at what goes on in your everyday life a bit differently. You may agree or disagree with what you read, but prayerfully you will not find anything that causes you to doubt your beliefs or feel like your beliefs are being questioned or are unrealistic.

I wrote this book out of a need to express my thoughts and life lessons with you. I felt a strong desire to share what I have experienced, learned and cherish with anyone who will take the time to read through this book. My hope is that as you read through these pages, you can open your mind and heart to receive and ponder the relevancy of the text.

In this book, in no specific order, are thought provoking paragraphs, poems, statements, scripture quotes from the New Kings James Version (NKJV) and the New International Version (NIV) of the bible and stories for your reading pleasure. So, since you've come this far, open the book and get started.

Enjoy!

Jo Ann

Acknowledgements

This collection of short stories and poems was divinely inspired and cultivated. I first thank God for the inspiration and for giving me the boldness to encourage others through His word, through my own life journey and my own life experiences.

Many, many thanks go out to my family and friends for allowing me to use portions of their history to compile this collection.

My prayer is that you will be encouraged just a little, that you ponder just a little, that you smile just a little and that you think of me just a little as you read through these pages. Be Blessed!

JoAnn Wilson

TABLE OF CONTENTS

"Light Inspires Life"

"TODAY"

"New Day"

"Don't Sit on It"

"Are You Living on Purpose?"

*"What Do You Do
When You Don't Know What to Do?"*

"Love-giving"

"Woe Is Me?"

"Opinions Matter"

"Miracles"

"God's Love"

"Me Time"

"EVERY NOW AND THEN – LAUGH"

"Music - How Sweet the Sound"

"Lessons Learned"

"Fighting Back"

"I Won't Take a Chance!"

"Isn't It Funny"

"The Beauty Within"

"I've Heard It All Before"

"So True"

About the Author – JoAnn Wilson

Light Inspires Life

"No one, when he has lit a lamp, puts *it* in a secret place or under a basket, but on a lampstand, that those who come in may see the light." *Luke 11:33 (NKJV)*

Light (noun) - The natural agent that stimulates sight and makes things visible.

Life (noun) - the quality that distinguishes a vital and functional being from a dead body

So then, what is this all about, *"Light Inspires Life?"* Think about how you feel when darkness turns to day, when cold becomes warmth, when heaviness turns to joy. In the spring, no matter how harsh the winter, new life begins - the weather gets warmer, the grass begins to sprout and flowers begin to blossom.

Think about the birth of a child, from the darkness and shelter of the womb, to a world of warmth, safety and love by the embrace of a loving mother.

Remember the relief you felt when a burden was lifted - the weight was gone and you felt light and alive again.

Just some examples of light inspiring life. The Bible reminds us that after you light a lamp, you put it on a table to illuminate things so all can see. Light gives you clear vision, hope and direction. A world that seemed so tiny in darkness is now filled with inspiration, new joys and new aspiration.

Light inspires life. Light inspires us to try again, to live again, to realize that you can be more, do more - to LIVE!

Most importantly is your relationship with God the Father, the giver of life, our creator who sent His only son that we may have life.

"For God so loved the world that He gave His only begotten Son, that whoever believes in Him should not perish but have everlasting life." *John 3:16 (NKJV)*

"Then Jesus spoke to them again, saying, I am the light of the world. He who follows Me shall not walk in darkness, but have the light of life." *John 8:12 (NKJV)*

Jesus' light gives life that the world cannot give. It's forever, unlike the world's light which is temporary. When you have that special relationship with Him, you will still have trials, troubles, tests and more, but you also have Him to talk to, cry out to and give your weight to. He promises to make things work for our good if we will only trust Him, hope in Him and wait for His timing. You and I know that when we are going through, none of this is easy, but His word is true.

"Trust in the Lord with all your heart,
And lean not on your own understanding; In all your ways acknowledge Him, And He shall direct your paths." *Proverbs 3:5 -6; (NKJV)*

"I called on the Lord in distress; The Lord answered me *and set me* in a broad place. The Lord *is* on my side; I will not fear. What can man do to me?" *Psalm 118:5-6 (NKJV)*

"I would have lost heart, unless I had believed that I would see the goodness of the Lord in the land of the living. Wait on the Lord; Be of good courage, And He shall strengthen your heart; Wait, I say, on the Lord!" *Psalm 27:13-14 (NKJV)*

There is so much more evidence in the Word of God to aid you through life's most challenging times. His light will give you the kind of life that is so much more than you could ever dream of or imagine.

Does light inspire life? Yes, it does! If you will turn on the lamp in your heart, you too will begin to see through the shroud of darkness and be inspired to enjoy life!

The Brightest Light is the Light Within You!

Ponder This

TODAY

This is Your Day – Make it count!

Today is the first day of the rest of your life. No, it's not your birthday, it's not New Year's Day and it's not any other special day; it's today. It's now.

Yesterday is gone; you can't change or rearrange it. Gone, done, over. It's today that counts, and it's a great beginning for hope, for recreating yourself. Yesterday, whether good or bad, is gone. If it was good, then build on it; you can do it! You have to make the choice that today is what matters.

Today the ball keeps rolling toward that prosperous future. If yesterday was not one of your best days, then learn from it; don't dwell on it. Find the lesson in the pain of yesterday and make the decision that yesterday won't keep you from the positive momentum of today.

Today is a new season in your life. Today gives meaning to the phase "new mercies/new grace". You didn't have a choice of whether or not you would see today, so be grateful for the opportunity to look life straight in the eye and determine you will go on. Give thanks for today, for a chance to be a blessing to someone else. Choose to be happy even when you hit the bumps in the road – and there will be bumps. Realistically, there will be highs and there will be lows and you have to make the choice that the lows won't take you out.

Today is your day and this is your time, so make it count – walk into your season!

Ponder This

_____
_____
_____
_____
_____
_____

New Day

Welcome, welcome brand-new day,
The rain is gone, the clouds have rolled away,
All I can see is sunshine everywhere,
I'm free from worry, free from care.

The ground is dry, the breeze is blowing,
The air is clean, the flowers are growing.
My mind is clear, my joy has returned,
This day is mine and there's no time to burn.

No looking back on the things that had me down,
No looking back at the people who made me frown.
No looking back on what was lost yesterday,
No looking back and being afraid.

Today is a welcome release from yesterday's woes,
Today I'm not worried about any of my foes.
Today my heart is full of God's unmerited Grace,
Today I feel like I CAN run another race.

Today I'm starting with a brand-new outlook on life,
Today is where I begin to get rid of misery and strife.
Today I begin to dream again,
Today my energy won't be drained.

I'm keeping positive thoughts in my head,
I'm refusing to let negative thoughts take the lead.

I'm keeping satan and his imps at bay,
I'm not giving them one inch of room to play.

It hasn't been easy, and it's going to be hard,
But I intend to move forward and take full charge.
Too long have I sat in the background and watched days come and go,
But, today is the day I take control and not go with the flow!

I'll take charge of my mind and let go of the past,
I'll do something different, and all I can ask,
Is for God to go before me and lead the way,
Then I'll know my direction is right and I won't go astray.

Yes, yesterday is gone; it's a brand-new day,
And I choose to live my life in a brand-new way.
I choose to live my life filled with hope and joy,
I choose to live life with fervor like never before.
I choose compassion and love over anger and hate,
I choose to lift up and not to berate.
I choose not to mope about what I can't change,
I choose to not to give in and not to complain.

Today I won't blame or find fault with anyone else,
Today I'll only look for the best in myself.
Today is a brand-new day, today is a new start
Today I'll set a new goal and try to reach a new mark.

I'll work while it's day to do my very best,
I won't let doubts rule, remembering they're only a test.
I'll put my best foot forward, with my head to the sky,
Trusting and believing things will work out, if I only try.

And what I don't finish today, only means one thing,
When the day dawns anew, I'll start all over again.
I'll start each brand-new day with purpose in mind,
I'll live as best I can, leaving yesterday behind.
Knowing my life will be richer, fuller and more blessed,
Knowing that with my gift of twenty-four hours, I've given it my best!

<u>Ponder This</u>

_____
_____
_____
_____
_____
_____

Don't Sit on It

Dancing to minister to God's people, writing a best seller, owning your own business – childhood dreams that were never realized, never accomplished. What happened to the excitement and the passion you once had? You knew exactly what you wanted to do and how you were going to do it. Every time you closed your eyes, you could see yourself living out your dream. Being young, money wasn't even the main objective; it was just doing that special thing that made you feel good. You had no idea how you were going to accomplish the dream; you just knew in your heart that the dream was what you were meant to do.

Somewhere along the line, your dream got dimmer and dimmer as you grew, aged and matured. You lost the passion you once held for your dream. Now, you probably have a great job, making a great salary and living a good life. You most likely have a wonderful family, good friends and many stimulating extra-curricular activities that keep you busy, but every once in a while, you have a fleeting memory of that childhood dream and wonder - what if?

What if you hadn't forgotten about the thing that gave you the most joy? What if you remembered how good you felt when you thought about what you were going to do when you grew up? What if you were given encouragement by family, friends and other important people in your life to follow your heart and go for it? Is it possible you could revive your dream? Is it possible? Is it possible you could do what many have doubted you could do? Is it possible you could believe in yourself enough to try? Is it possible? Are you dead –NO and of course, it's possible!

In a very familiar children's book, *The Little Engine That Could*, by Watty Piper, the main theme is *"I Think I Can"*. Sure, there was a little doubt when the little locomotive was asked to perform a mighty task and yes, he didn't feel like or thought he was qualified for the job, but with a lot of determination and a lot of effort, the little locomotive did. And so, can you! Sure, you're an adult and you might think that your childhood dream is silly now. Why would you put yourself in a position to be laughed at, ridiculed, criticized or even take the chance of having people wonder if you've lost your last mind? Why, because that gnawing feeling in your gut won't leave you alone, that's why!

Don't get me wrong, I'm not even suggesting that you throw everything away that you have worked so hard for and earned to go after a childhood dream. What I am suggesting is that you consider ways to incorporate your dream into your lifestyle, into your adult way of thinking. All I am suggesting is that you think about it. I am suggesting that you pray about it. Is there any way you could carve out a few minutes in your day to at least focus on the dream? Is your dream so unrealistic that it would be impossible for you to even try to achieve it? Have you prayed about it? Have you **really** prayed about it? Have you talked to God about it and have you listened for His answer? You do know that God works in ways not common to our finite minds and that He will not only speak directly to you, but He will also speak through people and things to get your attention. Do you have ears to hear and eyes to see the answer you are looking for? People are always quoting Philippians 4:13 – you know it well - "I can do all things through Christ who gives me strength". My question to you is, do you ***really*** believe it? Can you do it? Can you realize your dream, or will you continue to sit on it?

If you are perfectly happy with your life, then I am happy for you. If you have accomplished everything you ever wanted to achieve, then you are one-in-a-million, and I salute you. But, if there is something in the deep recesses of your mind that runs through every once in a while, then why not go for it? You may not be able to see the dream come to fruition like you saw it when you were younger and you may have to alter the end result to fit who you are now, but please don't sit on it. There is something about that sense of accomplishment, knowing that you never gave up on something that was once so important to you. Does it matter what people will think? Only if you go after something harmful to yourself or someone else.

Read *"The Little Engine That Could"* again to remind yourself of what you can do. I think I can, I think I can, I know I can, I know I can!

Ponder This

Are You Living on Purpose?

Have you ever stopped and wondered what would have happened if your steps had not been ordered by the Lord? If you had not listened to His still small voice, the voice that whispered go forth. Would you be living on purpose, fulfilling the vision God has for your life?

Supposed you had not been obedient to the will of Father God and had not taken the proper course, living a life of indifference, with your mind as your only guiding source? Would you be living on purpose, fulfilling the vision God has for your life?

What if you had not learned that everything belongs to God and had not obeyed His command to return to Him the first fruits of all your rewards? Would you be living on purpose, fulfilling the vision God has for your life?

What if you had not learned why you were created and what life holds for you? What if you had not invested the time to learn what you are really are called to do? Would you be living on purpose, fulfilling the vision God has for your life?

What if you didn't work on your relationship with God, didn't read His word, didn't fast or pray? Suppose you didn't commune with Him, every single day. Would you be living on purpose, fulfilling the vision God has for your life?

What if you didn't fellowship with other believers, to be strengthened through good times and bad? Would your life be the same or would you be lonely, unfulfilled and sad? Would you be living on purpose, fulfilling the vision God has for your life?

Can you answer the questions and can you honestly say yes? Do you know your purpose and do you know which path is best?

What is the vision and have you set a goal? In this grand scheme of life, what is your role?

Believe in yourself, the vision is clear,
God gave you the dream, there's no need to fear.
Live for today, hope for tomorrow,
Yesterday's gone, don't live with sorrow.
Live for someone less fortunate than you,
Live for that person who doesn't know the truth.
Live for that person who has yet to meet,
The only real One who can put new a new step in their feet.
Live to make a difference, show the world the power within,
Your life is a blessing, so give as much as you can.
Be a blessing to others so future generations will know,
That dreams can come true, if you believe and let go!

You were born for a reason – It's called PURPOSE!

Ponder This

_____
_____
_____
_____
_____
_____

What Do You Do When You Don't Know What to Do?

Sometimes in life, things get turned upside down. You're trying to go right, but the waves seem to push you left. You need to get to the tenth floor, the elevator is broken and the up escalator is out of order, so you have no choice but to walk up ten flights. What do you do – you need to get there (wherever your "there" is), but all you get are roadblocks. What do you do – push back. You've heard it before P.U.S.H. – Pray Until Something Happens.

Prayer works, if you believe and don't doubt. Satan, your mind, sometimes friends and even family will try to steer you in the wrong direction. Satan will whisper that no matter what you do, God has given up on you and pushed you to the curb. Your mind will tell you that Satan is right and provide the proof. Well-meaning family and friends will gently encourage you to give up on your dream, to try something else. What do you do? Will you be like Abram and just go? Are you like David, who sought the Lord in all situations? Will you trust like Jesus and say "not my will, but Thy will be done"? Will you pray without ceasing?

What do you do when you don't know what to do? Turn inward. Turn to the One who planned your life from the beginning of time. Have you developed that relationship with Him to be able to go to Him when all seems hopeless? Your loving Father will hear your petitions. He will dry your tears. Turn inward to that place where only God can touch. Go to Him. Talk to Him. Be honest and humble yourself. Seek Him with everything you have. He's waiting to hear from you. He already knows your situation, but won't overstep His boundaries. He needs you to ask for what you need. He needs you to pour out your heart to Him. He needs you to trust Him. He needs you to be patient, knowing that He has all the answers. He needs you to wait on the still, small voice of truth, direction and hope. He needs you to believe in Him, in His power and in His love for you. You need Him and He needs you. Waiting is hard under the best circumstances and waiting on God to "fix it" isn't easy. When all is said and done, the wait will be well worth it. God will open doors you didn't even know existed. What do you do when you don't know what to do – turn to the One who knows exactly what you need and exactly what to do. Pray and then pray some more, do your best and let God do the rest!

Prayer Changes Things!

<u>Ponder This</u>

_____

_____

_____

_____

_____

_____

Love-giving

There are persons in our lives who have given their all to make sure we had everything we needed and a lot of what we wanted as we grew up. Most of these people weren't rich, they were just hard-working fathers, mothers and other guardians who wanted us to have the best life had to offer. They probably started out with the same hopes and dreams we have today - a family you love and that loves you, a career you love, a nice home, and the list goes on. So, they worked for years to achieve their goals and now they are at a point in their lives where they can no longer function as they once could. It may be that age, hard work and daily stressors have taken its toll on the body and mind.

Most of the time, health issues strike the major blow to people. Little by little, limbs don't function as they did twenty to thirty years ago. It seems like the brain won't let them remember things that are important and now, that healthy, robust person who did everything for you now needs you to do for them what they can't do for themselves. To see these persons deteriorate right before your eyes, invokes a myriad of emotions. At first you may feel anger and frustration because you don't understand why this person is acting so much out of character. They are depending on you for daily and business matters, they're not understanding or retaining things you're telling them and they are relying on canes and walkers for mobility purposes. Doctors confirm their declining health and your anger turns into realization that what the person is going through is really happening. Now you begin a new life style that includes caregiving.

Caregiving involves making sure that you supply the love and support for a person who can no longer perform daily life activities without assistance. Depending upon whether the person lives alone or in your home determines the type and amount of support you give. Depending on the type of issues they may have, you will have to determine if you can provide the proper support a person may need. Caregiving is more than you ever imagined or considered. Take a look at some bible passages regarding support:

"Honor your father and your mother, so that you may live long in the land the Lord your God is giving you." *Exodus 20:12 (NIV)*

"If any of your fellow Israelites become poor and are unable to support themselves among you, **help** them as you would a foreigner and stranger, so they can continue to live among you." *Leviticus 25:35 (NIV)*

"If either of them falls down, one can **help** the other up. But pity anyone who falls and has no one to **help** them up." *Ecclesiastes 4:10 (NIV)*

"In everything I did, I showed you that by this kind of hard work we must **help** the weak, remembering the words the Lord Jesus himself said: 'It is more blessed to give than to receive.' " *Acts 20:35 (NIV)*

"And we urge you, brothers and sisters, warn those who are idle and disruptive, encourage the disheartened, **help** the weak, be patient with everyone."
1 Thessalonians 5:14 (NIV)

"God is not unjust; he will not forget your work and the love you have shown him as you have helped his people and continue to help them." *Hebrews 6:10 (NIV)*

Caregiving is one of the many sacrifices you may have to make during your lifetime, but if you look at it from a different perspective, you find that you are doing what I like to call *"love-giving"*.

Love-giving involves more than supplying the outward needs of a person, but it also includes giving from your heart – you make it personal. When you consider who the person is, what the person represents in your life and the sacrifices they made so you could have a better life, love-giving seems only natural. You want to do everything you can to make that person feel loved, appreciated and protected, so you go to God and ask Him for guidance. With His help, you become patient, compassionate and tender. He will give you everything you need including wisdom and knowledge to help you care for that person. Don't be afraid to ask for help. God will direct you to persons and agencies that will be able to assist you.

Love-giving builds a new relationship. Roles change and now you have the responsibility of making necessary decisions and sacrifices for someone. You may not be able to go out like you used to. You may not be able to work long hours or you may not be able to go to work at all. You may have other family members that need your time and attention.

I implore you to put your trust in God. He will supply all your needs and the needs of the one you are caring for. He knows about the situation, and it is true, He won't put more on you than you can bear.

If you are in the medical field and give care as a professional, the same rules apply. You may not have a personal connection to the person you are caring for, but that person is relying on you to take care of them as though they are family. You should ask God to **help** you be the best love-giver you can be to that person also.

In all situations, whether you are a caregiver or a love-giver, whether family or patient, you and the person you care for are children of God. If the situation should arise, there is no other response other than do what Jesus would do.

"Finally, all of you, be like-minded, be sympathetic, love one another, be compassionate and humble."
1 Peter 3:8 (NIV)

Your Best Asset – Your Love for Others!

Ponder This

_____
_____
_____
_____
_____
_____

Woe Is Me

Sometimes I wonder "why I've been chosen to do what I do"? This is not the direction I thought I would be going in at this point in my life - no way! After working and retiring from two jobs, I thought I would be "taking the bull by the horns", so to speak. I assumed that I would be doing me; whatever I wanted, whenever I wanted. Ha, ha, ha, the joke is clearly on me! My life now consists of three major components which are taking care of mom, going to CVS, and going to the market.

Sometimes, I'm even able to go to a service on Sunday mornings. My house has never been cleaner. There are no clothes in the laundry baskets because I wash at least once a week – full load or not. I'm caught up on all my favorite shows. You can usually find me in evening attire or sweats because there is no sense putting on regular clothes just to walk around the house to do chores.

Would you like to come to my pity party? Right now, it's in full swing. It started right around the time the forecaster predicted inclement weather. I knew at that point I was going to be indoors for sure and not because of a major storm, but because of my current situation. Roads too bad to get out early and not enough time to get out and back by the time they clear. Still want to come to my party? I can go on if you want, but I don't think I will. I think right here and now, I'm going to change my way of thinking. Lights out, party's over!

You know, I am really blessed. God blessed me to be able to retire in time to be a blessing to my mom. As a child, I'm sure it was no easy feat for her to have to work a low-paying job to take care of a home and two children. Now, in her advanced years, I am thankful that number one, she's still here and two, I'm able to provide for her physical needs. You see, sometimes I need a reminder that this life I live is not all about me. Sometimes I have to be reminded that I was placed on this earth to give, not receive. Sometimes I forget my purpose is not about me, it's about how I can spread God's love to those He places in my path.

It's so easy to throw a pity party or go to a dark place when you focus on what you don't have, where you can't go or what you can't do. I've come to realize, that is exactly what satan wants us to do. Sure, when it's gray, it's easy to let doom and gloom fill your mind. If you suffer with depression or any type of mental instability, you are an easy target. What I've learned is that just because you have a "situation", that "situation" doesn't have to have you! If you're willing to fight for your mind, you can improve your "situation". Situations come in all shapes, sizes, colors, and individuals.

A situation usually comes about when you least expect it and can last longer than necessary or imaginable. You can bring on a situation or it can come out of left field. In any case, when you've got a situation, your world feels like its spinning out of control. Whether it's self-inflicted or handed to you by life, circumstances or other people, your situation can take full control of your life if you don't handle it properly. One thing is for sure, your situation is yours and you have to find the best solution for you to work it out.

For me, I've learned I have to reign in my thoughts. I have to take control of my mind and focus on the positive. I must take my eyes off the negative and put myself in God's capable hands. I have to believe and trust that He is totally aware of me and my situation. I must grab on to that mustard seed of faith and give my situation over to Him. I must listen for His still small voice that will lead me in the right direction. I must be obedient to His words and do as instructed. If I do these things, I find that my situation isn't as traumatic as I first believed. If I truly believe Romans 8:28, "And we know that all things work together for good to those who love God, to those who are the called according to His purpose," then I have to know that God will do just as He promises.

Back to my current situation and why I'm blessed. Though the weather forecaster called for inclement weather, I didn't have to worry about having to go out; whether to work, the market or any other place. I have a roof over my head, utilities are on and working and food to eat. See, sometimes we are so busy looking at our situations, we forget to look at our blessings. We tend to take so much for granted, that we don't appreciate that we have everything we need to survive and sustain us. Often, we don't appreciate when we have to slow down because we believe that the world will stop revolving if we aren't in attendance. Many times, we're so busy looking back, we can't see how we're being prepared for tomorrow. While we're trying to figure out how to get that "must have" thing, we don't realize that the thing we can't live without might be the very thing that will cause us to be in a dire situation!

Taking care of my mom has given me a greater appreciation for patience and compassion. Prayerfully, as I continue to grow in grace, if I get to the point where I am no longer able to take care of my own personal needs, I pray that those who may have to care for me will have the patience and compassion to assist me.

Caring for someone who can no longer care for themselves is one of the greatest ways you thank God for blessing you. Service to and for others is one of the best gifts you can give and is how you can get off the pity train fast.

So, in closing, when the train pulls up to your door and pity jumps off and tries to invade your space, say no thank you, gather your luggage and hop on board the glory train bound for joy, unspeakable joy!

You can't control what happens to you, but you can control your response!

Ponder This

_____
_____
_____
_____
_____
_____

Opinions Matter

Can we be serious for a second? When you come to me and ask for my opinion on a matter, do you really want my opinion, because that's what I'm going to give you, or do you just want to vent or blow off steam? If you ask me what I would do in a particular situation, do you really want to know what I would do in that situation? When you ask me what you should do about a problem, do you intend to access my words to determine if they will help or hinder you or have you already made up your mind about what you're you going to do?

Normally, I would feel honored to know that someone thinks so highly of me that my opinion, insight or recommendation on a subject would make such an impression on them that they would act on my words -- but most of the time, that is not the case. Although the person may have good intentions when they come to me, the truth is they really don't care about my opinion, wouldn't do what I would do nor do they feel how I would handle a problem is best for them. If you come to me, believe me, I am not going to just blow you off and give you an off-the-cuff response.

I have grown in many areas of my life, and maybe not as much in other areas. I admit I am not an expert on every conceivable topic and don't claim to be, however, I've come across many situations in my life that I have strong feelings on.

I've seen people go through some turmoil that could have been prevented if they had only looked before they leaped. I know people who are so impulsive – they act then think. These are good, hardworking people with little patience when their backs are up against a wall. I don't look down on them, belittle them or think any less of them – I pray for them. I'm not saying that your instincts aren't important, but acting on instinct and acting on impulse are totally different reactions. I believe that instinct is God driven and leads to a good outcome; impulse, however, is self-driven and usually ends with a negative result.

Look at it this way, we're all in this thing called life together and the main thing I've learned is that we need each other. We're here to be a blessing to those in need. I may not have dollars to dole out, but I can pray and ask God to step in your situation. Prayer is all powerful. Prayer is a tool we can all use. God is accessible to everyone. He is waiting to hear from us. I'm not saying that when trouble comes, you shouldn't do all you can to work things out. What I am saying is that after you've done all you can in the best, legitimate way, give it over to God.

What I will say is that trusting and believing in the One who created us, the One who already knows our situations and understands what we are going through, He is the One who is waiting for us to ask Him for help.

In My Opinion

You may get frustrated with me when I don't say what you want to hear and don't come up with what you need to fix your situation - well, I'm only human. You'll probably get frustrated with God when He doesn't work as fast as you think He should or even in the way you think He should. This is one opinion you can take to the bank - God can and God will if you will only ask, trust, believe and wait on Him. My opinion is - Whatever you're going through is only a test!

Ponder This

_____
_____
_____
_____
_____
_____

Miracles

Life is a Series of Miracles!

Ever wondered if you ever witnessed a miracle? How about that time when you thought all hope was lost, and then out of nowhere, you got exactly what you needed? You never imagined you could or would get the answer you needed and then it came in an extraordinarily strange or different way, for no plausible reason and better than you ever expected.

A miracle can be defined as an amazing event, a marvelous example, or an act of God. Miracles can happen to anyone, at any time and for any reason. Most of the time, we experience miracles every day and never take notice of the fact that a miracle occurred right in our midst. Every day you wake up is a miracle. You go through your daily routine without giving thought that in the blink of an eye, your life could change drastically for the better or worse – but what kept you safe are the miracles that happened in those twenty-four hours! How many times as a child were you injured, but not unto death – a miracle? How many times while driving, you avoided being involved in an accident either major or minor – a miracle? How many times have you thought to yourself, "It's a miracle......"

Several years ago, was the very first time I truly recognized a miracle for what it was. I had applied for several positions for which I knew I was highly qualified.

In my mind's eye, I began packing my luggage to go on to my next destination. Imagine my disappointment when I wasn't selected for any of the promotions! When I inquired as to why I hadn't been selected, I was told by my atheist supervisor *"many are called, but few are chosen"*. You know satan knows the bible and tries to reel you in when he thinks you're open. Upset and confused, I began to question my own self-worth. I continued to go to work and do my job, but I was feeling like I was in a hopeless situation. In desperation, one Thursday morning, when I felt I couldn't go to work another day pretending everything was okay, I fell on my knees and cried out to the Lord.

As I cried and poured out my heart to God, I suddenly felt weight being lifted from my knees, right up through my shoulders and out of my body. It was then my miracle began. I was freed. I felt light-hearted. My whole attitude toward my job changed. Within a month, my supervisor changed. My new supervisor let me know that she had responded to a request for a recommendation about me from a totally unexpected component. I never applied for a position there because I knew I would have never qualified for any position in that component. A few weeks later, I was promoted into that very position I had never heard of, in the component I knew very little about! Coincidence you say – I beg to differ – I called it a miracle! Now I look for miracles, not only in my life but in everything and everyone around me.

You've heard the expression hundreds of times – in fact, just about every time a woman gives birth, people refer to the newborn as a miracle.

In the early eighties, a song came out with the lyrics *"I'm looking for a miracle, I expect the impossible, I feel the intangible, I see the invisible."* My daughter, who was about two or three at the time, heard that song at one of the choir rehearsals we were attending and after that, on the radio. Well, that was all it took – for a whole year, she sang those lines over and over and over. As adults, we didn't believe this child understood the meaning of the phase she sang, but was just enjoying the beat of the music. So, life goes on. At twenty-three years old, in August 2004, she and the rest of my family witnessed the miracle she sang about so many years ago.

My daughter gave birth to Madi, a one pound, six-ounce, eleven inches long baby girl. Madi came into this world facing what seemed like insurmountable health challenges. A week after her birth, she had to have major surgery and then a second surgery to correct the first surgery. After that, she spent three months in the pediatric intensive care unit. Eventually, Madi came home on oxygen and soon physical and occupational therapy began. Now this little girl, our miracle, is a healthy, happy young lady who exudes love and joy wherever she goes and we thank God for her every day. I believe it's what took place immediately after her birth and continues to this day that bought her miracle about. Prayers were sent up from family, friends, anybody and everybody! At work, it was strictly forbidden to send emails across the "universe" unless it was work-related and you had authorization. Did I care or heed the restriction of using a government email server for private use – no, I didn't. I sent an email asking anyone who knew the worth of prayer and believed in God, to pray for Madi. The call went out around the world and the prayer warriors responded! Not only were the responses overwhelming, but I was never even reprimanded for sending the email - a miracle!

Miracles can happen at any age. As a child, my parents were divorced when I was a young girl. My mom did her best to support me and my sister. In the sixties, job opportunities for people of color were scarce, especially older women with no marketable skills, but my mom did find work and it was hard and tiring. Now, as a working, single mom of two, she didn't have time for doling out the sugary, sweet encouragement that usually comes from a mother who had time and finances to pour into her children. None-the-less, she loved us fiercely and did everything in her power to show it. I'm just saying that although I may not have been encouraged to pursue my dream, I was encouraged to do my best to become self-sufficient. It wasn't until my mom was in her late eighty's and I was in my early sixty's that the miracle happened. After reading some material I had written, my mother encouraged me to pursue my dream of writing. You would have to know my whole story to understand what that meant to me. Just to know that she actually believed that other people would enjoy reading my thoughts was awe-inspiring. A miracle!

God hears our prayers, knows the desires of our hearts, and provides the miracles we need. Yes, He already knows, but He still wants us to talk to Him. He is waiting to hear from us. He won't intrude, but He won't let you fail either. We take Him for granted. We take His mercy and grace for granted. We take His miracles for granted.

He doesn't owe us anything, but we owe Him everything! Think about it, do you really believe you are a self-made person? You really believe you can make it on your own merits? Did you wake yourself up this morning? Did you create all that you can touch, feel or imagine? What about your peace of mind – did you know how to get it?

I find it easier to believe that there is someone who loves me so much and wants the best for me so much that He would provide miracles to get my attention, just so I can be happy. Just so I can trust. Just to have a little conversation with me.

Think back over your life and you won't be able to count all the miracles that happened to and for you. You know, all those times you said "whew" and never thought to utter a thank you to God. Those times when your breakthrough came and your life changed forever. All those miracles you never knew about, imagined or expected.

Life itself is a miracle. Every breath you breathe is a miracle. Nothing happens to you without God's permission! Now you know, so there's time to change your thought process. Take time every day to thank the

One who created the universe. He is the same God who supplies your miracles. Your life may not have turned out the way you thought it would – it may be wonderful or you may be struggling, but remember every morning you get to enjoy a brand-new day and you need thank God for creating a new miracle for you!

Ponder This

_____
_____
_____
_____
_____
_____

God's Love

"For God so loved the world that He gave His only begotten Son, that whoever believes in Him should not perish but have everlasting life." John 3:16 (NKJV)

You learned this scripture as a child and somewhere hidden in your heart and soul it remains to this very day. God's love is just awesome. Your situation, although it may not be the best right now, could be a whole lot worse – except for God's love. In this season of love, go back to your roots and remember that you are not alone, you are loved. You can hope in the great and mighty love of the One who loved you from the beginning of time.

He's your Savior and Redeemer! He's never left you! He's going through everything you're going through, even carrying you when necessary; so, don't forget – your family loves you, your church family loves you, your friends love you, but there is no love greater than the love of your Heavenly Father. Feeling helpless, hopeless or unloved – remember this – there is no greater love in heaven above or earth below than the love of your Creator, your Keeper, your Hope and Your Peace – the lover of your soul – God the Father, God the Son and God the Holy Spirit! Accept His love, embrace His love, and live in the knowledge that no matter what it looks like, you are loved!

God Loves You!

Ponder This

_____
_____
_____
_____
_____
_____

Me Time

Writer's block. Sometimes I want to write, to express myself, but the thoughts just don't come together. There is so much going on in my head that I can't focus on any one particular issue. Family, friends, work, home, finances, this, that, and the other all vie for top spot in my mind. I don't believe that I'm the only one this happens to. I've heard and read about people who couldn't move toward their dreams and goals because they felt blocked or stifled, you might say, by the rumblings in their mind. They wanted to go forward, but the energy it would take to move just wasn't there, so they allowed themselves to stay stuck behind a wall of complacency, excuses, and feelings of hopelessness.

I get tired of not doing what makes me feel good about me. I often feel the desire to achieve more, to do more. To be perfectly honest, I need more than my everyday routine of doing the same thing from morning until night; not that my routine is bad or unrewarding, it just doesn't include much me time. Me time, the time I need to spend alone with me, myself and I to find me again. Me time, the time I need to regroup so that I can be a better me. Me time, the time I need to remember who I am and what I want out of life. Me time, the time I need to listen to what the Spirit is trying to tell me without Him having to cut through the clutter in my head. Everybody needs me time. Everybody needs that space in their daily twenty-four hours to take a break from everything that's going on in their world; to slow down to relax, relate and release. Ten or fifteen minutes a day will open you up to a side of yourself that you forgot ever existed. Those few minutes will re-energize you and help you to reconnect with you.

So, how do you get that much needed me time? You just have to take it! You have to stop what you're doing and take a few minutes to recharge your batteries. If you are determined enough, you will find those precious few minutes to get back to you. Easy for me to say – not. I have to carve out my minutes just like you. I may have to sacrifice something on my to-do list to do what I need to do for me. When I'm not busy with the have-to's of my daily routine, I take my me time. No, it's not easy, but it is necessary – for my sanity's sake.

Who knows you better than you? When you're forced to be like the Energizer Bunny and keep going and going and going, what happens to you? Do you turn into some monstrous person who nobody wants to be around? Do you become aloof and unresponsive? Guess what; even the bunny needs to have his batteries recharged to keep going.

Don't be fooled by the commercial – everything and everyone runs out after a while - and so will you! I finally got it (an aha moment) and you will too. Carve out that 'me' time. You'll be surprised how you'll feel and even how much better you're able to cope with your daily stressors when you give yourself a break.

You don't have to do it all, and if you are honest with yourself, you can't do it all, even on your best day. Giving yourself a minute or two makes things clearer. Having ears to hear what the Spirit has to say to you helps you learn how to deal with people and situations that may seem unusually stressful. Writer's block certainly does exist, but clearing the muddy waters helps crumble those blocks piece by piece just a bit faster.

And guess what? After a while, you'll start to get greedy. A few minutes of me time won't give you the results you're looking for. Yes, a few minutes of me time really does help, but the truth is - *YOU NEED MORE*. You have to have more. You feel it so strongly within you that it's like you're gasping for air. If you don't get more, you feel like you're going to explode – not something you want or you want anyone in your space to experience. Yes, it's necessary – emotionally, physically and spiritually necessary.

So now you have to plan for more me time – a couple of hours, a day, a weekend. Take yourself to a nice restaurant and have lunch. Go see a movie that you want to see without having to explain why you want to see it. Go for a good laugh or a good cry.

Schedule that long overdue massage and let someone rub the tension out of you with some soothing oils and good music. Go bowling and picture those pins as some stressors in your life. Go to a hotel, let Calgon take you away and wallow in some cushy, comfortable pillows and silky, soft sheets. Spend some time in the midst of God's creation by sitting in the park, walking through a beautiful botanical garden or driving through a mountain path lined with trees. Whatever your mind can conceive as relaxation, go for it and be a little selfish.

Things probably won't fall apart while you're away, but they aren't going to be any better with you there and in a bad mood either. Be brave and just go for it!

Stop putting yourself on the back burner and start finding ways to get rid of that writer's block. Pray about it. Ask God to show you how and when to find time for you. The truth is, you probably haven't really connected to Him in a while either. You know that He is the perfect one to show you where you can get exactly what you need. As a matter of fact, if you start your few minutes of me time with God, you'll find that He'll show you chunks of time and space you never imagined existed! Conquer writer's block with me time – you deserve it!

Ponder This

_____
_____
_____
_____
_____
_____

EVERY NOW AND THEN – LAUGH

It's ok, really!

Laugh out loud!

"He that is of a merry heart has a continual feast."
Proverbs 15:15 (NKJV)

Laugh with friends!

Laugh when you feel like crying.

Don't trust anyone who doesn't laugh.

Laughter is good for the soul

Laugh at jokes

"For His anger *is but for* a moment,
His favor *is for* life;
Weeping may endure for a night,
But joy *comes* in the morning."
Psalms 30:5 (NKJV)

Ponder This – I Laugh Because

_____
_____
_____
_____
_____
_____

Music - How Sweet the Sound

"Let the message of Christ dwell among you richly as you teach and admonish one another with all wisdom through psalms, hymns, and songs from the Spirit, singing to God with gratitude in your hearts." *Colossians 3:16 (NIV)*

I love music, just about every genre, but Christian and Gospel are my favorites. Music does something to my spirit – it quiets me and calms me. Music helps me to reflect on where I've been, where I am in the now and where I'm going. Music helps me worship and give praise. There are certain songs that I listen to over and over just because the messages are so powerful.

Sometimes if I'm lonely or afraid, I am reminded that I have a friend in Jesus who is always there. It's at those low times that I realize that I shouldn't feel discouraged or lonely because Jesus watches over me.

I'm reminded that I'm safe and loved because of Psalm 23.

But still, because I'm human, I go through rough patches and my spirit is low. Sometimes I realize I haven't talked to my Father in a while, but I know I can call on Him and His love will comfort me.

When I'm tired of fighting and worn out because of the endless battles that seem to be raging in my life, it's then that I throw my hands up and surrender all to Him. While I'm wondering and waiting to see if God is going to come through for me, I get that knowing feeling deep in the pit of my belly that tells me if He did it before, He will do it again.

Yes, Jesus loves me, for the bible tells me so. He thought enough about me to die on a cross - how awesome is that!

> Holy, holy, holy! Lord God Almighty!
> Early in the morning our song shall rise to Thee;
> Holy, holy, holy, merciful and mighty!
> God in three Persons, blessed Trinity!
>
> Holy, holy, holy! All the saints adore Thee,
> Casting down their golden crowns around the glassy sea;
> Cherubim and seraphim falling down before Thee,
> Who was, and is, and evermore shall be.
> *Written by Reginald Heber (1783–1826)*

Finally, I know that along the way, the road may be bumpy, but I'm going to press on and enjoy this journey because God's will shall be done. I'm not who I used to be and I'm not everything I'm supposed to be, but I am a work in progress and God is perfecting me every day.

Pondering on music blesses my soul. Open a hymnal and let the words fill your spirit. Turn on the radio or listen to your favorite CD. Go to your playlist and reminisce on those melodies that will turn your frown upside down, that will have you humming along and that will cause you to tap your feet.

Music – How Sweet the Sound!

Ponder This

Lessons Learned

As time passes and you know that it will,
Memories and thoughts your mind does fill.
Lost loves, missed chances, dreams and hopes have died,
Now, all that's left is a morsel of pride.

You made a choice, you took a chance,
That leap you took just did not last.
So, what do you do, what did you learn,
You paid the price, but those bridges are burned.

Deep down inside, you ponder and muse,
Reflecting on the past and what you can use.
To further your career, to begin again,
The fight's not over, you're going to win.

Considering what worked and what went wrong,
A new game plan is in the works, and it won't be long.
You'll be back in the race, back on your feet,
With positive thoughts and deadlines to meet.

The future's looking brighter; things are falling into place,
Now, slow down a bit, and move at the right pace.
Be honest, be sure of what you need to do,
Go to the Source, He'll see you through.

Is that what happened the last few times,
You tried it on your own, and didn't seek His face?

You had plans and they fell through,
Didn't you know He has plans for you?

Plans to prosper you, to give you hope and a future,
To make your days brighter because you're not a loser.
If you only learned one thing from your past mistakes,
Make sure that you learned to go to God first,
He knows what's at stake.

The road may not be easy; no one said it would be,
But with God as your leader,
Lessons learned, past forgotten, you are an achiever!

The Best is Yet to Come!

Ponder This

_____
_____
_____
_____
_____
_____

Fighting Back

It's 12:15 a.m. in the morning, and for the first time in a long time, I feel the need to put my thoughts on paper. To be perfectly honest, the last few months of my life have been up, down, around and back, but it's time for the something fresh and new.

In the past few months, my only daughter got married, which was a most joyous occasion, so I've gained a son and additional grandchildren. I've worked at a part-time job and retired for the second time to take on the responsibilities of becoming a full-time caregiver for my mom, which includes taking her to necessary doctor's appointments and provide for her daily needs, in addition to being a part-time chauffeur for my number one granddaughter. Life has been busy. While I've had time to exercise a little more and clean my house from top to bottom, it's funny that I haven't been able to carve out my life as I had planned.

I had planned on spending more time at the gym, getting involved with a senior group, write more often and I planned to chill whenever I wanted. These things seem like innocent, practical ideas, but they aren't working out as planned. The only thing I can come up with is that God must have another plan for this season of my life. My obedience to Him is my first priority and I take it one day at a time, trying my best to listen for His still, small voice which I know and believe leads me down the right path.

Being the thinking person that I am, I often hesitate to make quick decisions because I try to make sure that the decisions are best for everyone involved. What I quickly learned is that I'm not going to please everyone, so I stop trying. I finally got it through this thick skull that my joy and happiness come from being who I was created to be and that it all begins on the inside. I find some time to focus on me - I am fighting back; which means I am fighting for what I want and for the person I want to be - joyful, happy and full of peace. Fighting back means finding time during my day to concentrate on God, read and meditate on His word and understand His purpose for my life.

I've learned that my time with Him makes my days a little easier to get through, no matter how challenging they may be. See, being open with you, I want to share with you that I suffer with depression. I'm no longer ashamed to admit it because I know there are many others like me facing this same reality. Unlike many who are afraid of facing ridicule from people who don't understand this disease, I rely on God's grace and mercy, medication and the support of friends and family, to deal with this illness. I have special people I can go to, talk to and relate to when symptoms come on. They understand me because they go through the same things.

When the negative thoughts rear their ugly head, these are the folks I can go to for help to turn those negative thoughts into positive thoughts and actions. I have learned that although I have depression,

depression doesn't have me, doesn't own me and can no longer control me!

There is another valuable lesson I've learned in my life and it's about control. I can only be in control of me and no one else. When I give up control of my mind and spirit over to people, especially those who don't have my best interest at heart, that's when I begin to drown in negativity. It's at that point when thoughts of unworthiness and hopelessness begin to fill me and I begin to lose control. On the other hand, when I stay in control and shut out the negative voices, focus on God, think positive thoughts, reach out for help when necessary and take my prescribed medication, I am actually capable of fighting the good fight. It's at that point when my life takes a turn for the better, my mind clears and sharpens and I can then focus on God, hope, faith and positive goals.

Just putting these thoughts down on paper and opening up have given me hope. With everything going on in my life right now, I didn't think I would ever be able to express my feelings, but God is good! He knows what you need and when you need it. To sit here and reflect on where I've been and where I am headed, I know I won't be throwing a pity party any time soon.

If nothing else, I know this one thing - God really does love me and He is still keeping me in the hollow of His hand. With His help and guidance, I am going to do what I need to do and allow Him to do what I can't. I know that greater is coming and it's only because of Him, so I'm going to fight back and praise Him now because not only is He an awesome God, but He is truly worthy to be praised!

Ponder This

_____
_____
_____
_____
_____
_____

I Won't Take a Chance!

I won't take a chance of giving up now,
It's been too hard to keep my hand to the plow.
I won't take a chance of losing it all,
For a moment of fun that may cause me to fall.
I won't take a chance and not swallow my pride,
If it means I'll lose what I've gained inside.
You see the pleasures of life may seem fun at first,
But time will pass and the bubbles will burst.
When things begin to spiral out of control,
You'll grab at thin air, because there's nothing to hold.
When money is gone and friends are few,
When trouble hits home and you don't know what to do,
You'll ask yourself why this would happen to you.
Oh, you already know you went down the wrong path,
But you thought you were the one who could make it last.
Then the bottom fell out and your confidence went with it,
No matter how hard you tried, you just couldn't fit.
So, after trying everything you could think to do,
And talking to those who you thought were true blue.
You finally came to yourself,
And put your pride back on the shelf.
You called on the name that is like none other,
The One who is closer than any other brother.
He picked you up and wiped your tears,

He held you close and you knew there was nothing else to fear.
He made your pain cease to exist,
He turned your sorrow to joy with a flick of His wrist.
So, now your world is right again,
Because the Savior did what only He can.
That's why I won't take a chance of losing what I've found,
Peace, joy, wisdom and love now abound.
I'm in a place I've never been before,
I won't take a chance reopening that closed door.
This life I now live is filled with something new,
There's a bright horizon in my view.
No, I won't take a chance and go back to my old ways,
And I'll continue to worship and give Him all the praise.
Without His love and patience with me,
I would never be who He created me to be.
No, I won't take a chance, not anymore,
I won't, I just won't, and of that I am sure!

Ponder This

_____
_____
_____
_____
_____
_____

Isn't It Funny

Isn't it funny you get the urge to move - at the strangest time?

Isn't it funny that all of a sudden, everybody's calling your name for one thing or another?

Isn't it funny how when you are quite comfortable where you are; and then bam—out of nowhere, the shoe drops!

Isn't it funny you're working today and laid off tomorrow – with no prior warning?

Isn't it funny how your spouse has decided that the marriage is over –without even discussing it with you?

Isn't funny how that child that you put on a pedestal, is now disrespecting you?

Isn't it funny how you miss one car payment and now they're ready to repossess your vehicle?

Truth is – none of these things are funny. There is no humor in pain, loss or disappointment. You are mad! You really want to hurt somebody! You want to tell somebody off! You want to set the record straight, because evidently, they've got the wrong person and they are about to get hurt!

So, you go into attack mode and start planning how to retaliate; how are you going to hurt that person who hurt you? You start looking for avenues to get your shot in, but for some reason, the right opportunity never seems to come up.

What are you going to do now – lay in wait or leave it alone and move on?

"Beloved, do not avenge yourselves, but rather give place to wrath; for it is written, "Vengeance is Mine, I will repay," says the Lord. *Romans 12:19 (NKJV)*

Isn't it funny, your Daddy won't let you mess up His plans?

Isn't it funny that before you were in relationship with Him, you could come up with a comeback as quick as you could snap your fingers?

Isn't it funny how He will turn your pain, sorrow and loss into joy?

Isn't it funny that when you hold your peace, you then find peace that surpasses all understanding?
Isn't it funny how God, who loves you so much, with all your mess, sees you as a palm tree, bending but not breaking?

Isn't it funny that you won't trust Him, after all the times He's turned things around for you, changed your situation, picked you up, dusted you off and cleaned you up, that you still don't believe He can handle everything thrown at you.

Isn't it funny?

Put Your Broken Pieces in the Potter's Hand and Let Him Put You Back Together Again!

Ponder This

_____
_____
_____
_____
_____
_____

The Beauty Within

You smile when you want to cry, you're quiet when you want to scream, you make the extra effort when you want to say no. You are strong when you should, could or want to be weak. You have stamina when you're exhausted and drained and it all comes from the beauty within.

You listen when you're tired. You talk when you just want to be quiet. You get up too early and go to bed too late. You take care of family, the home, the friends and more and it all comes from the beauty within.

Shining like millions of beams of light in darkness, the beauty within glows, strengthens and empowers you to do what you have to do, what you need to do. The beauty within comforts those in need. The beauty within radiates love and support to those around. The beauty within is the outpouring of God living in you, and for that – count it all joy!

You Are So Beautiful!

Ponder This

_____
_____
_____
_____
_____
_____

I've Heard It All Before

At home, momma's saying the same old things,
Get your butt up off the floor,
Be proud, be strong,
Don't get involved with the wrong crowd and you think
- I've heard it all before.

On Sundays when you go to church and hear the pastor preach,
Stop doing this,
Stop doing that,
Change your ways,
Change your attitude,
Give God a chance to change your life; and you think –
I've heard it all before.

In school, the guidance counselor implores you to bring your grades up,
Do your homework,
Excel in your studies, but are you really listening?
Are you gonna make some changes?
Or are you just thinking – I've heard it all before.

So, why does everyone keep harping on the same old things?
You're not doing so bad,
You've settled into a comfortable lifestyle,
You're staying under the radar,
You're not making any noise,

You're just existing, but it's just not working and you wonder why;
Why? Because you heard it all before.

So, why not put yourself out there?
Why not give it another shot?
What do you have to lose?
Sure, you've heard it all before, but were you really hearing?

There's life after pain,
There's life after doubt,
There's life after failure,
Are you really listening?

Be strong, be brave,
Take the first step into a new world,
A world of hope, a world joy, a world where dreams do come true,
Are you really listening?

It takes hard work, I kid you not,
It takes determination,
It takes humility to begin at the bottom,
But, you can do it,
Are you really listening?

Are you listening to the compliments?
Do you realize you have talents, skills and abilities?

Somewhere in this great universe of ours, someone needs what you have to offer,
Pick yourself up, go for it and just do it!

You may need to go back to school,
You may need some additional training,
You may need to get your head on straight,
Pick yourself up, go for it and just do it!

It's never too late to make a fresh start,
Believe it or not, there are more for you than are against you,
So, you've heard it all before,
But, were you really listening,
Today is the day to start believing in you,
Pick yourself up, go for it and just do it,
You'll be amazed at what you can achieve!

Don't Just Dream About It – Take Action!

<u>Ponder This</u>

_____
_____
_____
_____
_____
_____

So True

Through the years, I've heard many, many words of wisdom and have learned many lessons that have proven to be true and well worth remembering. Some sayings are from the bible, some from wise persons, some from celebrities, some from regular people and some from my own life experiences. So, I am just wondering - how many can you relate to - hmmm?

- ❖ Tough times don't last, tough people do.
- ❖ It's only a test.
- ❖ Trust God!
- ❖ Weeping may endure for a night, but joy comes in the morning. *Psalms 30:5 (NKJV)*
- ❖ Your first instinct is usually right.
- ❖ When you put God first, things fall into place.
- ❖ If at first you don't succeed, try, try, try again!
- ❖ Every day is a day of thanksgiving.
- ❖ Trust God!
- ❖ Be very careful who you tell your dreams to.
- ❖ Seasons change, so do you!
- ❖ If you always do what you've always done, you'll always get what you've always got.
- ❖ Your attitude determines your altitude.
- ❖ Wishing doesn't make it happen!
- ❖ Trust God!

- ❖ Stop thinking about it, Do It!
- ❖ There will be setbacks!
- ❖ Believe in yourself!
- ❖ Stop procrastinating!
- ❖ Surround yourself with positive people
- ❖ Holding a grudge is like letting someone live rent-free in your head.
- ❖ Don't lose sleep over the opinions of chickens - Think like an eagle!
- ❖ You are responsible for your own life!
- ❖ Enjoy life to the fullest – it has an expiration date.
- ❖ Trust in the LORD with all your heart, And lean not on your own understanding; In all your ways acknowledge Him, And He shall direct your paths. *Proverbs 3:5-6 (NKJV)*
- ❖ Be anxious for nothing, but in everything by prayer and supplication, with thanksgiving, let your requests be made known to God; 7 and the peace of God, which surpasses all understanding, will guard your hearts and minds through Christ Jesus. *Philippians 4:6-7 (NKJV)*
- ❖ Nobody said it would be easy.

There are so many other sayings, scriptures and words of wisdom you have probably heard, live by and could add to this list. These are just a few of my favorites that I refer to time and time again when I feel the weight of the world on my shoulders and I need some relief. I hope and pray that you find some insight, peace and encouragement in one or two of the above to help usher you along the path of life you have been ordained to follow. If you'd like, please jot your favorite(s) on the lines below and you ponder this. There's nothing like a written word to jolt you back from a dark place!

Peace Out!

Ponder This

_____

_____

_____

_____

_____

_____

About the Author – JoAnn Wilson

For more than six decades, JoAnn Wilson, who was born and raised in Baltimore, Maryland, has made Baltimore her forever home. She received her education in the Baltimore City Public School system and took various college courses at several local universities. JoAnn's professional career began and ended in the Federal government. Now retired after thirty-seven years of public service, JoAnn is enjoying church, her family, friends and past-times which include traveling, sewing and her love of writing.

JoAnn's love of writing led her to participate as a contributing writer in several compilation writing projects. Her works can be found in the *One Sister Away: Encouraging Words From One Sister to Another*, book series, Volumes 2 and 3 and in the heart-touching book, *A Letter to My Mother*, where she paid tribute to her mother.

About the Publisher

CRBarton Productions is a company dedicated to helping writers become authors. Our foundation is based on the belief that there is a writer in all of us and that there are people who would love to read what we all have to say. Get moving toward that dream today!

Our company motto is, "Your Dreams Are Safe in Our Hands" and we stand behind that.

Our CEO, Cheryl Barton, is a published author who has written and self-published over twenty novels. She brings all that she has learned in writing and publishing her own novels to the table when it comes to helping other writers fulfill their dreams.

For more information on the services provided by CRBarton Productions and to see other book selections, visit our website at www.crbarton.com.

Made in the USA
Columbia, SC
15 May 2018